seasonal
cupcakes

CAROLYN WHITE

David and Charles

Celebrate with cupcakes!

From spring into autumn and then on into the winter, the fun way to mark the changing of the seasons and celebrate the key occasions is to make a special collection of cupcakes. These little cakes are perfect to set the scene or create a centrepiece for a party, or simply serve them as an entertaining family treat. Prettily packaged, they are also ideal for gifts or for guests to take away with them. The cakes taste delicious too, and the bases and frostings can be mixed and matched and used for any project you choose to decorate them with – or enjoy them just as they are for an everyday bite.

This book has been devised for those new to making cupcakes as well those who are looking for fresh design ideas and decorating techniques, and as a helpful guide each project has a difficulty rating indicated by one, two or three cupcake symbols.

So make your seasonal celebrations extra special by re-creating these characterful and colourful cupcakes, and you may soon be inspired to develop your own designs!

Contents

Tools & equipment

Before you start, it's a good idea to check you have everything to hand that you might need. Included in this section is a list of essential equipment for making and baking your cupcake sponge bases and to whip up your frostings; a basic decorating toolbox; and key specialist tools. Don't feel you need to have all the latter kit to create fun cupcakes, but if you are making a large quantity or get really hooked, these are the items I find really useful. Specific tools required beyond the basics are listed under 'you will need' at the start of each project.

Baking essentials

★ Kitchen scales/measuring cups and measuring spoons – for accurately weighing ingredients

★ Electric stand mixer with paddle attachment (flat beater) – to make the sponge cake base and toppings

★ Muffin and mini muffin trays (pans)

★ Wire rack – to cool cupcakes

★ Flexible plastic spatulas – for scraping out bowls

★ Muffin baking cases (liners) – keep a variety of the many fantastic designs available, both paper and foil, on hand for spontaneous events

★ Large disposable plastic piping (pastry) bags, 46cm (18in) and 53cm (21in) – for piping your mixture into cases

★ Oven thermometer – a must if unsure of your internal oven temperature

★ Microwave or double boiler – for melting chocolate

★ Plastic or glass microwave-safe bowls – for melting chocolate and butter

★ Sieve (strainer)

We usually use muffin or mini muffin-size baking cases (liners) because they are just the right size to be flat frosted to present your cupcakes beautifully and still give a perfect amount of sponge. Smaller cupcake or fairy cake cases are not suitable for these projects.

Basic decorating toolbox

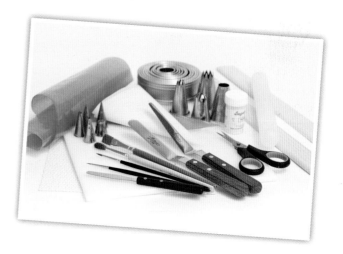

★ Non-stick work board with non-stick mat beneath to prevent slipping – to roll out icing and cut out and model paste shapes

★ Non-stick rolling pin – for rolling out sugarpaste (rolled fondant) and flower (petal/gum) paste

★ Icing spacers – to get an even 3mm (⅛in) thickness

★ Large disposable plastic piping (pastry) bags – for piping frostings

★ Paper piping (pastry) bags – made from baking (parchment) paper for small quantities of royal icing/ applying details

★ Piping tubes (tips) – fine for piping royal icing details; large for piping frosting

★ Scissors – to snip the ends of piping (pastry) bags for piping tubes (tips) to fit snugly

★ Large and mini palette knives – large for buttercream; mini for cutting, turning paste and lifting paste shapes/ features

★ Paintbrushes – a selection of sable (no. 3 for glue) and pony (no. 8 for edible shimmering flakes, non-toxic glitters and lustre dusts) are handy for all sorts of details

★ Set of 11 circle cutters (Ateco) – nos. specified count outwards from the smallest, no. 1

★ Icing smoother – for smoothing and polishing sugarpaste (rolled fondant)

US cup measurements

If you prefer to use cup measurements, please use the following conversions. (Note: 1 Australian tbsp = 20ml.)

liquid
1 tsp = 5ml
1 tbsp = 15ml
½ cup = 120ml/4fl oz
1 cup = 240ml/8½fl oz

butter
1 tbsp = 15g/½oz
2 tbsp = 25g//1oz
½ cup/1 stick = 115g/4oz
1 cup/2 sticks = 225g/8oz

caster (superfine) sugar
½ cup = 100g/3½oz
1 cup = 200g/7oz

icing (confectioners') sugar
1 cup = 115g/4oz

flour
1 cup = 125g/4½oz

chopped nuts
1 cup = about 125g (4¼oz)

Specialist decorating items

★ Shaped cutters – ovals, hearts, square, star, triangle

★ Kemper mini plunger cutters – 4mm (⅛in) circle and heart; PME blossom set comes with a foam pad to push plunger against to cup the paste

★ Ball tool and smile tool (PME) – for adding detail to paste characters

★ Dresden tool – for scoring lines into paste and adding texture

★ Paint palette – for mixing colours and blending gold/ silver lustre dust with alcohol

★ Dusting brush – for brushing lustre dust onto paste

★ Cocktail sticks (toothpicks) – for making tiny indentations and applying colour to icing

★ Foiled cake board – for storing made-ahead paste discs

Cupcake recipes

My team and I always use a stand mixer and where possible give easy 'all-in-one' recipes, but if you wish to make your cake mix by hand, cream the fat and sugar together in a mixing bowl with a wooden spoon until light and fluffy before gradually beating in any liquids and finally incorporating the flour with a large metal spoon.

Classic vanilla

Light and luscious, this vanilla sponge recipe will never fail to produce a great sponge base for the most fabulous decorations. If you fancy a change for a more zingy flavour, simply follow the suggestions for a citrus version.

you will need...
makes about 12

* ★ 125g (4½oz) margarine, softened
* ★ 125g (4½oz) caster (superfine) sugar
* ★ 1 tsp (5ml) vanilla extract
* ★ 2 eggs (medium or large), lightly beaten
* ★ 125g (4½oz) self-raising (-rising) flour
* ★ 2 tbsp (30ml) milk

1 Preheat the oven to 200°C/fan 180°C/400°F/Gas Mark 6. Line your muffin tray (pan) with muffin cases (liners) and set to one side.

2 Place the margarine, sugar and vanilla extract in the bowl of an electric stand mixer and cream together until light and fluffy.

3 Add the eggs gradually, then sift the flour into the mixture and combine on a low speed. Add the milk until you have a smooth dropping consistency.

4 Spoon the mixture evenly into the cases or fill a large disposable plastic piping (pastry) bag with the batter, snip off the end and pipe into the cases.

5 Bake for 25–28 minutes, or until risen and springy to the touch. Cool on a wire rack.

To vary the flavour of the sponge, for lemon or orange, replace the vanilla extract with a teaspoon of lemon or orange oil. For a more zingy citrus taste, add the finely grated zest of one washed unwaxed lemon or orange. For a chocolate chip option, add 100g (3½oz) dark (semisweet or bittersweet) or milk chocolate chips.

Double chocolate

If you want a really good, dependable chocolate cupcake recipe, this is the one. The cakes keep well and are great for decorating, but they are also ideal just with a cream cheese frosting or a decadent chocolate frosting.

you will need...

makes about 12

* 112g (4oz) butter, cut into pieces

* 75g (2¾oz) dark (semisweet or bittersweet) chocolate callets or pieces

* 150g (5½oz) caster (superfine) sugar

* 60g (2¼oz) self-raising (-rising) flour

* 1½ tbsp cocoa powder (unsweetened cocoa)

* ½ tsp baking powder

* 3 large eggs, beaten

1 Preheat the oven to 190°C/fan 170°C/375°F/Gas Mark 5. Line your muffin tray (pan) with muffin cases (liners) and set to one side.

2 Put the butter and chocolate in a microwave-safe bowl and place in a microwave oven on low for about 2 minutes, checking often, until melted. Stir in the sugar and then leave to cool.

3 Meanwhile, sift the flour, cocoa powder and baking powder together into the bowl of an electric stand mixer.

4 Add the eggs along with the melted chocolate mixture to the dry ingredients. Beat on the slowest setting and then increase the speed gradually for 2–3 minutes, or until well combined.

5 Using a spatula, fill a large disposable plastic piping (pastry) bag with the batter, sniff off the end and pipe into the muffin cases, or spoon the mixture evenly into the cases.

6 Bake for 20–25 minutes, or until risen and springy to touch. Cool on a wire rack.

Cupcake troubleshooting

Some cooked but others not quite – the oven may have a hot spot, so the muffin tray (pan) needs to be rotated around halfway through baking time

Dense or heavy texture – mixture not thoroughly mixed together and the raising agent hasn't been distributed evenly; can also be caused by overbeating

Banana & macadamia

These cupcakes are tantalizingly exotic tasting, with their tropical fruit, rich nuts and warm spice. You can also use natural (plain) yogurt or sour cream instead of the buttermilk.

you will need...

makes 12–15

- ★ 210g (7½oz) plain (all-purpose) flour
- ★ 1 tsp bicarbonate of soda (baking soda)
- ★ ¼ tsp salt
- ★ ½ tsp ground cinnamon
- ★ ⅛ tsp allspice
- ★ 125g (4½oz) unsalted butter, softened
- ★ 300g (10½oz) caster (superfine) sugar
- ★ 2 large eggs
- ★ ½ tsp (2.5ml) vanilla extract
- ★ 100ml (3½fl oz) buttermilk
- ★ 1–2 overripe bananas, depending on size, mashed
- ★ 60g (2¼oz) macadamia nuts, chopped

1 Preheat the oven to 170°C/fan 140°C/325°F/Gas Mark 3. Line your muffin trays (pans) with muffin cases (liners) and set to one side.

2 Sift the flour, bicarbonate of soda, salt and ground spices together into a bowl.

3 Place the butter in the bowl of an electric stand mixer and cream for 1–2 minutes. Add the sugar and beat together until the mixture is light and fluffy.

4 Add the eggs one at a time, beating for 1 minute after each addition, or until the mixture is light and fluffy. Add the vanilla extract and beat until combined.

5 Add a third of the flour mixture to the creamed mixture and mix on a low speed until combined. Add half the buttermilk and half the mashed banana and mix until combined, then repeat this process. Add the remaining third of the flour mixture and beat until thoroughly combined; do not overbeat as this will toughen the mixture. Add the nuts and beat again until evenly combined.

6 Spoon the mixture evenly into the cases. Bake for 20 minutes, or until a fine skewer inserted in the centre of a cake comes out clean. Cool on a wire rack.

Cupcake troubleshooting

Peaked – either too much raising agent or the oven temperature is too hot

Sunken – not cooked for long enough or oven door opened too soon

Sloping – check with a spirit level that your oven shelves or even the oven itself is level

Topping recipes

A cupcake is nothing without its finishing touch of decadent frosting, and there are lots of sumptuous recipes to choose from here to suit a variety of tastes.

Royal icing

Royal icing is used in small amounts to pipe eyes and fine details, and also to fix embellishments. You can make your own, described below, or use a commercial powder mix. You can use fresh egg white or dried egg powder. If you are using a dried powder, add water and soak for a minimum of 40 minutes or even overnight in the fridge. When ready to use, strain the mixture first.

you will need...

★ 500g (1lb 2oz) icing sugar

★ 2 egg whites, or 15g (½oz) dried egg albumen powder mixed with 75ml (2½fl oz) water

1 Sift the icing sugar directly into a bowl and add the fresh egg whites or strained soaked dried egg whites. Using an electric mixer, mix slowly on a low speed for 5 minutes until the icing has reached a 'stiff peak' stage.

2 It is now ready to use or store. It can be stored in the fridge for 2–3 days covered with cling film (plastic wrap) and in a lidded box. To colour the icing, simply add some drops of colouring with a cocktail stick (toothpick) and mix well, adding more drops until the shade is as you desire.

Save time by keeping a box of ready-made royal icing powder in the store cupboard. You can make up very small amounts and use immediately. Just follow the manufacturer's instructions.

Buttercream

This is what my kids love more than anything – sweet, fluffy buttercream just piped in a swirl as the finishing flourish to an irresistible cake! For really generous swirls of vanilla buttercream, simply double the quantities listed.

you will need...

Vanilla

★ 250g (9oz) lightly salted butter, softened

★ 500g (1lb 2oz) icing (confectioners') sugar

★ 2½ tbsp (38ml) water

★ ½ tsp (2.5ml) vanilla extract

Chocolate

★ 250g (9oz) dark (semisweet or bittersweet) chocolate callets

★ 500g (1lb 2oz) salted butter, softened

★ 500g (1lb 2oz) icing (confectioners') sugar, sifted

Vanilla

1 Place the butter in the bowl of an electric stand mixer. Sift over the icing sugar.

2 Add the water and vanilla extract and beat on a slow speed, then increase the speed to high and beat until light and fluffy.

Chocolate

1 Put the chocolate callets in a plastic jug. Place in a microwave oven on low for 2 minutes, checking often, until melted.

2 Place the butter and sugar in the bowl of a stand mixer and cream on a slow speed. Add the melted chocolate and beat on a high speed until soft and light.

For a lemon buttercream, add a little good-quality lemon oil to taste, and for an orange buttercream, finely grate the zest of one washed unwaxed orange and mix into the buttercream.

Whipped chocolate frosting

I love this frosting as a lighter alternative to ganache. It's great for kids as it is more buttery – plus it's so easy to make. Either spread directly onto your cakes with a palette knife or spoon into a large disposable plastic piping (pastry) bag fitted with a piping tube (tip) and pipe on.

you will need...

★ 200ml (7fl oz) double (heavy) cream

★ 150g (5½oz) plain (semisweet) chocolate, finely chopped or callets

★ 280g (10oz) icing (confectioners') sugar, sifted

★ 140g (5oz) unsalted butter, softened

1 Place the cream in a microwave-safe bowl and heat in a microwave oven until boiling. Add the chocolate and stir until smooth.

2 Leave to cool for 30 minutes, stirring occasionally as it thickens.

3 Place the sugar and butter in a separate bowl and beat until smooth, then beat the cooled chocolate mixture into the butter mixture. Chill for 25 minutes.

Chocolate callets is the term for high-quality Belgium chocolate, which I always use in preference to ordinary chocolate bars. The chocolate comes in small buttons that melt quickly without burning or splitting and produce the best flavour, so always try to use these if you can.

Applying frostings

Most of my cupcake designs have a buttercream or a frosting topping added before the final decoration. Check that your cupcakes are appropriate for the method of frosting – if they are too peaked or high, a flat finish won't work, so use a swirl of frosting instead, or re-bake with less mixture in the case! All the cupcakes will taste great even if you choose to have some with just frosting on top for a more adult treat along with others that are fully decorated.

Flat frosting

A flat fill is a really useful technique to master, as it can provide a great blank canvas for presenting a whole variety of sugar decorations and piping. Alternatively, you can place a cut-out disc of sugarpaste (rolled fondant) on the flat surface.

1 Take a full palette knife of frosting and spread around to fill the case.

2 Then sweep the knife straight across the top of the cake, removing any excess, to give a completely flat top.

3 You can then add piping and decorations to the centre, as in the bunny and chick cupcakes (**see Easter: Bunnies and Chicks**), or place a disc of sugarpaste directly on top.

Dome frosting

A half-sphere dome of frosting is required for some of the cupcakes, such as the spider (**see Halloween: Scary Spiders**) and plum pudding cupcakes (**see Christmas: Rudolph and Friends**), and an extra-tall mound of frosting for the ghost cakes (**see Halloween: Spooks**).

1 Using a palette knife, build up a mound of the frosting on the cupcake, adding more until you have the height and width you want. Use the knife to roughly shape the frosting into a dome.

2 Dip the knife into boiling water and quickly smooth the icing – it will take off any roughness. You must work quickly here, as you don't want to melt the frosting!

Piped frosting

For beautiful swirls of frosting, it's well worth practising before piping for real. Cut the tip off a large disposable plastic piping (pastry) bag and drop your chosen piping tube (tip) into the bag. Always only half-fill the bag with the frosting so that it doesn't leak out. Eliminate any trapped air and then twist the open end of the bag closed, apply pressure and begin to pipe onto the cupcake.

Piped swirl

1 Working from the outside inwards, pipe one complete swirl.

2 If you end up with a peak of icing in the centre, tap the cake down sharply on the work surface.

Piped raised swirl

1 To create a cone shape, as for the Christmas tree (**see Christmas: Oh Christmas Tree**), start near the centre and pipe upwards in a tight gradual spiral.

2 Build up on the layer before to bring the frosting up to a peak.

recommended piping tubes (tips)

no. 10 open star – great for piping a general swirl

no. 828 open star – for an alternative general swirl

no. 808 plain open round – used for the Santa's hats (**see Christmas: Festive Favourites**) and great for no-fuss swirls

no. 1B drop (WIL) – used for creating the Christmas trees (**see Christmas: Oh Christmas Tree**)

no. 233 – used for creating grass and bird's nests (**see Easter: Bunnies and Chicks; Nest of Eggs**)

Using sugarpaste

You can make your own sugarpaste, but it's easiest to buy ready-made. For all the projects I have added CMC (carboxymethyl cellulose) to sugarpaste, a synthetic gum that adds elasticity and strength. This effectively turns it into modelling paste, which you can buy ready-prepared but it's preferable to add CMC to sugarpaste so that you can use pre-coloured pastes yet give them that extra flexibility and strength desirable for sugar decorations.

To make up a batch of sugarpaste with CMC, use 1 tsp CMC per 225g (8oz) sugarpaste. Make a well in the sugarpaste and knead in the CMC. If using small amounts of different colours straight from the packet, just pick up a tiny amount of CMC on the end of a palette knife and knead in. The paste will start to firm as soon as the CMC is incorporated so that it can be used straight away. Knead it well before using to make it warmer and thus more pliable. It will continue to firm over the next day and then remain firm. Store it in a plastic bag.

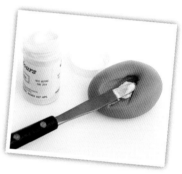

Covering with sugarpaste

I love the look of sugarpaste (rolled fondant) placed directly onto cupcakes. Just follow these simple steps to ensure a neat, professional result.

1 Using a palette knife, apply a little buttercream directly to the sponge surface to adhere the paste.

2 Knead the sugarpaste until it is warm and flexible, then roll it out using a non-stick rolling pin on a non-stick work board (with a non-stick mat underneath to prevent slipping). Place icing spacers either side of the paste you are rolling and keep rolling until the pin is rolling on the spacers evenly and your icing will then be a level 3mm (⅛in) thickness.

3 One of my most useful tools is a set of various sizes of circle cutter – select the most appropriate size for your cupcake and cut a circle.

4 Use a palette knife to lift the paste and place on top of your cupcake. Use the palm of your hand to smooth the paste into position. Trim off any excess with the palette knife if necessary.

Making sugar glue

Although you can easily buy a pot of sugar or edible glue, I prefer to make my own glue so that I can manage the consistency, creating a firm or looser glue depending on what I need to use it for. The synthetic gum CMC is used for this purpose too.

To make a batch of sugar glue, you need to make a blend of 1 part CMC to 20 parts warm, previously boiled water. Pick up the CMC on the end of a mini palette knife and place in a small screw-top jar. Add the water and stir. Leave with the lid off for 40 minutes to allow the glue to thicken. If you wish to make it the evening before, screw the lid on and leave in the fridge overnight to activate.

Colouring sugarpaste

I tend to use commercially colour-mixed pastes as they have been scientifically balanced not to be too dry or sticky to work with, but you can add colouring to white sugarpaste instead. Apply a gel paste colour with a cocktail stick (toothpick) so that you don't add too much colour at any one time, and use plastic gloves to stop the colour dyeing your hands bright green or red – you can get some funny looks when you forget to use gloves!

If making a dark colour, to prevent the paste turning sticky from the large amount of gel paste colour needed, add a pinch of CMC and leave the paste in a plastic bag for 10 minutes to firm a little.

Colouring other icing

For colouring frostings, such as buttercream, I usually use gel paste colours. But remember to take into account the colour of your frosting, which can affect the colours you add to it, for example the natural pale yellow of buttercream will make a light red colour look quite orange or pink, or a blue colour take on a greenish tinge.

For colouring royal icing, use droplet food colours for making pale colours and gel paste colours for creating much deeper tones or black.

Colour blending

To create a specific colour such as deep purple, you can start with a purple-coloured paste and add extra gel paste colour to it. However, I prefer to blend different pre-coloured pastes, such as purple and navy blue, which makes a really vibrant deep purple.

It's a good idea to experiment with blending colours, as it saves you having to stop and mix each individually – just take a pinch or ball of each colour such as red and yellow, then simply knead together and you have orange!

Presentation, display, storage & transportation

There are lots of exciting ways to present your decorated cupcakes, whether as an eye-catching display or for a special gift, so it's worth taking time to consider the various creative options.

Wherever possible I try to create decorations and even cupcakes ahead of time so that on the day I only have to whip up the frosting and put them all together. This isn't possible for every design in the book, but where you can it's the best approach to adopt, as it takes the stress out of the occasion and makes it all the more fun! Just take care and plan for storing and transporting your cupcake creations.

Cupcake stands

These look fantastic even before you add the cupcakes! Available as single layers or in tiers in a variety of designs and materials such as china, Perspex, wire or acrylic, they are perfect for creating a professional display at parties and special events.

Large cupcake gift boxes

Cardboard cupcake boxes have a tray with multiple holes cut into it for keeping the cupcakes in position and a clear lid, making them great for presenting a whole collection of cupcakes as a gift.

Single cupcake gift boxes

There are lots of individual cardboard cupcake boxes available with clear lids, as well as clear plastic boxes that can be dressed with ribbon, which are ideal for when you want to present single cupcakes as a special gift or for guests to take home with them.

Cupcake wrappers

These are a simple way to add a bit of fun to your cupcakes, and there are designs for every occasion, from spider's webs for Halloween to snowflakes for Christmas.

Storage containers

It's important to use the appropriate container to maintain your cupcakes and/or cake decorations in tip-top condition.

Airtight plastic storage boxes – these are great for storing cupcakes if you bake them the night before, or even to freeze them in.

Cardboard cupcake boxes – these are ideal for storing your decorated discs or decorations, as they allow a limited amount of air to circulate around them during the drying process while keeping them in a dust-free environment. Don't use plastic containers, as they cause the icing to sweat.

Safe transit

If you need to transport your cupcakes, make sure you package them up in the right way to protect them and ensure that they arrive in perfect shape.

Plastic 'cupcake' caddies – some are stackable and have multi-layers that are great for transporting cakes.

Cardboard cupcake boxes – this is the very best way to transport your cupcakes, each having its own little hole to sit in so that the cakes don't slide around. You can stack the boxes to make them easy to carry.

Easter

These cupcakes are just bursting with the joys of
spring! There are fluffy-tailed bunnies and cutesy,
sunny yellow chicks, along with pretty dainty
blossoms to brighten up your Easter table. And with
clever use of a must-have multi-holed grass-effect
piping tube, you can easily create lush green grass
and chocolate twig nests to hold sugar eggs.

Design inspiration ideas

It's easy enough to vary the ideas here to create other Easter
designs. In place of the dainty blossoms, cut out some bold
daisy shapes or daffodils, or make Easter bonnets along the lines
of the Witches' Hats (see Halloween) but using brown paste
and forming a domed crown – you could even texture them for
a straw effect. Or cut out colourful oval egg shapes instead of
bunnies and chicks and have fun embellishing them.

Difficulty rating:

Nest of eggs

Realistic chocolate nests with sugar eggs – present them with the Easter bunnies and chicks for a spring-themed celebration.

you will need...   makes 12

* 12 cupcakes flat frosted with chocolate frosting

* 400g (14oz) chocolate frosting

* sugarpaste (rolled fondant) with CMC: 40g (1½oz) each lilac, pink and yellow

* white royal icing in paper piping (pastry) bag with no. 1.5 piping tube (tip)

* sugar-coated chocolate eggs

* no. 233 grass-effect piping tube (tip)

* blossom plunger cutter set (PME metal or plastic)

1 Pop the grass-effect piping tube into a large disposable plastic piping (pastry) bag and fill with the chocolate frosting.

2 Pressure pipe a circle around the edge of the cake to build a rim of chocolate twigs for containing your bird's eggs.

3 Use the smallest two blossom plunger cutters to cut out flowers from the sugarpaste colours. Pipe a dot of royal icing in each flower centre. Leave to dry.

4 To finish, decorate with a few blossoms and place the sugar eggs in the centre of the nests.

mini nests...
Try creating mini versions for mouth-size holiday treats.

Recipes cupcake • topping   **Techniques** applying frostings • using sugarpaste

Chirpy chicks

These cheery chick cupcakes are perfect for the Easter holiday – try mixing them with mini-cupcakes of speckled eggs nestled among the spring flowers.

you will need...   makes 12

* 12 cupcakes with piped swirl of frosting

* sugarpaste (rolled fondant) with CMC: 250g (9oz) bright yellow, a little orange and pink or lilac

* black royal icing in paper piping (pastry) bag with no. 1.5 piping tube (tip) or black edible pen

* sugar glue

* cutters: 3.5cm (1⅜in) heart, mini blossom plunger

1 For the chick bodies, roll out the yellow sugarpaste to 3mm (⅛in) thick using spacers. Use a circle cutter (about no. 7) to cut 12 circles to fit your cupcakes.

2 For one pair of feathered wings, roll out the remaining yellow sugarpaste a little thinner than before. Use the heart cutter to cut down once into the paste and lift the excess paste away. Rotate the cutter slightly and cut down a second time so that you cut away some of the existing paste to create a three-pointed wing shape. Repeat to cut a second wing. Position either side of the body, then use the circle cutter from Step 1 to cut down and trim the edges of the wings. Attach in place with a little sugar glue.

3 For the beaks, using a sharp knife, cut 12 small triangular shapes freehand from thinly rolled-out orange sugarpaste. Using a mini palette knife, lift up and position on the faces, then attach with sugar glue. For the eyes, pipe two medium-size dots of black royal icing above the beak quite close together, or use a black edible pen.

4 To finish off your chicks in springtime style, use the plunger cutter to cut 12 dainty blossoms from very thinly rolled-out pink or lilac sugarpaste, then attach one to the top of each chick's head to one side. Roll tiny balls of yellow sugarpaste and glue one to the centre of each blossom.

flower power...
Other cupcakes in the set could be decorated just with the pretty blossoms dotted over the swirl of buttercream.

Recipes cupcake • topping   **Techniques** applying frostings • using sugarpaste

Difficulty rating:

Bunnies and chicks

Here, cute bunnies are pictured hopping away with their sugar tails disappearing through the lush green grass, while little yellow chicks gambol.

you will need... makes 12

* 12 cupcakes flat frosted with Party Green (SF)-coloured vanilla buttercream

* flower (gum/petal) paste: 50g (1¾oz) teddy bear brown, 30g (1oz) pale lemon

* white royal icing in paper piping (pastry) bag with no. 1.5 piping tube (tip)

* sugarpaste (rolled fondant) with CMC: 40g (1½oz) each lilac, pink and yellow

* 300g (10½oz) Party Green (SF)-coloured vanilla buttercream

* cutters: bunny set (PME), chick set (C4F), blossom plunger set (PME metal or plastic)

* no. 233 grass-effect piping tube (tip)

* black edible pen

1 Use the bunny and chick cutters to cut out cut out 12 each large and smaller bunnies from the brown flower paste and six chicks from the lemon paste. Use the white royal icing to pipe a round tail onto the bottom of each bunny and an eye on each chick. Leave to dry.

2 Use the smallest two blossom plunger cutters from the set to cut out flowers from the sugarpaste colours. Pipe a dot of royal icing in each flower centre. Leave to dry.

3 Use the no. 233 piping tube in a large disposable plastic piping (pastry) bag to pipe small clumps of the pale green buttercream on top of each green flat-frosted cake, varying the heights. Leave to dry.

4 Add a dot of black edible pen to the chicks' eyes. Add the chicks to six of the cakes and the bunnies to the remaining cakes with blossoms.

summer scene...
Take this design into summer by decorating the grass with deckchairs, flip-flops or footballs, or even fairy toadstools.

Recipes cupcake • topping **Techniques** applying frostings • using sugarpaste

24

Halloween

Frighten and thrill the adults as well as the children with these suitably spooky cupcake designs – just the thing for upping the atmosphere and entertainment value at a trick or treat event. Techniques involved include simple piping, using cutters, scoring with a Dresden tool and creating a gleaming gold metallic effect.

Design inspiration ideas

Extend your Halloween collection with other equally creepy concepts. Rather than spiders, mould black paste into swooping bat shapes with outspread wings, or create a skeleton from separate pieces of white paste. For a really stomach-turning design, roll pale paste into eyeball shapes, add a sickly green paste iris and black pupil, then coat with edible clear gel and add veins of red food colouring for a slimy, bloodshot look.

Difficulty rating:

Pumpkin faces

These creepy cakes will make a big impact on Halloween with their bold colour and dark and nasty crooked smiles.

you will need... makes 12

☾ 12 cupcakes with half-sphere dome of frosting

☾ sugarpaste (rolled fondant) with CMC: 500g (1lb 2oz) orange, 100g (3½oz) green, 40g (1½oz) black

☾ sugar glue

☾ Dresden tool

☾ 1cm (½in) triangle cutter

1 Roll out the orange paste to 3mm (⅛in) thick using spacers. Use the largest circle cutter to cut a circle. Smooth over a dome-frosted cupcake and use a palette knife to trim the excess paste just below the case (liner) top. Use the Dresden tool to score six evenly spaced lines from the outer edge to meet at the centre top.

2 For the stalk, roll a green paste sausage, stand upright and smooth downwards and outwards to widen the base. Score with the Dresden tool and curve it slightly. Attach with sugar glue.

3 For the eyes, use the triangle cutter to cut two triangles from the black paste. For the nose, cut another black paste triangle and trim off the base.

4 For the crooked smile, use a no. 4 circle cutter to cut a black paste circle, then use a no. 6 circle cutter to cut across it to create a crescent shape. Use a sharp knife to cut away two small sections top and bottom. Attach the features in place with sugar glue.

more grisly grins...
You can vary the shapes of the features to make different evil-looking expressions – why not try using pumpkin carving kits as a source of inspiration.

Recipes cupcake • topping Techniques applying frostings • using sugarpaste

Difficulty rating:

Ghoulish mummies

Get ready for some spine-chilling thrills in the form of these ghoulish mummies. You can have fun changing their eye colours to make them individually alarming!

you will need...   makes 12

- ☾ 12 cupcakes with half-sphere dome of frosting

- ☾ sugarpaste (rolled fondant) with CMC: 1kg (2lb 4oz) white, 100g (3½oz) black, 40g (1½oz) yellow

- ☾ sugar glue

1   For the bases, roll out the white paste to 3mm (⅛in) thick using spacers. Use the largest circle cutter to cut 12 circles. Smooth over the dome-frosted cakes and use a palette knife to trim the excess paste just below the tops of the cases (liners).

2   Cut black paste bands and attach to the cake fronts where the eyes will be. Cut eyes from yellow paste freehand. Attach tiny slightly flattened balls of black paste for pupils.

3   Cut the remaining white paste into long, narrow strips. Brush with sugar glue and attach to the cakes to resemble bandages, allowing the eyes to peak out, crossing them over in places and leaving the odd end loose.

all stitched up...
To add some super-scary realistic detail, you could run a stitching tool along the edges of some of the bandages to resemble a line of stitches.

Recipes cupcake • topping   *Techniques* applying frostings • using sugarpaste

Difficulty rating:

Scary spiders

These great big black spiders are crouching in wait, webs at the ready, to ensnare any unsuspecting Halloween trickster. So eat them up quickly to be safe from their clutches!

you will need... makes 12

(12 cupcakes with half-sphere dome of frosting

(sugarpaste (rolled fondant) with CMC: 500g (1lb 2oz) green, 500g (1lb 2oz) black, 40g (1½oz) white

(Extra Black (5F)-coloured royal icing in paper piping (pastry) bag with no. 1.5 piping tube (tip)

(sugar glue

(mini circle plunger cutter

1 For the bases, roll out the green paste to 3mm (⅛in) thick using spacers. Use the largest circle cutter to cut 12 circles. Smooth over the dome-frosted cakes and use a palette knife to trim the excess paste just below the tops of the cases (liners).

2 For the web, use the black royal icing to pipe six evenly spaced lines running from the edge to edge over the centre top of the cake. Then pipe two lines to horizontally link the web sections.

3 For the spider body, roll about 10g (¼oz) of black paste into a ball. For the head, roll about 7g (generous ⅛oz) into a ball.

4 For the eyes, roll small balls of white paste, flatten slightly and attach to the head with sugar glue. Use the mini plunger cutter to cut black paste circles and attach as pupils.

5 For the legs, roll a long, narrow rope of black paste and cut into 3cm (1¼in) lengths, eight for each spider. Attach the head and body in place on top of the web, then apply sugar glue to the underside edge of the body where you want the legs (applying the glue at this stage allows time for it to react with the paste and become really sticky). Bend each leg about 1cm (½in) down its length and pinch the bend into position, then attach the 1cm (½in) section to the body by easing it into the glued spot – it should adhere straight away.

make it easy...
Try using an icing smoother when rolling the black paste for the legs, as it will help you to roll long, smooth and narrow ropes with ease.

Recipes cupcake • topping **Techniques** applying frostings • using sugarpaste

Difficulty rating:

Spooks

What better treat for the tricksters at Halloween than these spooky cupcakes – haunting ghosts with their horrid hollow eyes and gaping mouths!

you will need...   makes 12

(12 cupcakes with extra-tall dome of frosting

(sugarpaste (rolled fondant) with CMC: 100g (3½oz) black, 1kg (2lb 4oz) white

(sugar glue

(mini circle plunger cutter

1 Use a no. 3 circle cutter to cut 12 black paste circles and attach to the front of each tower-frosted cupcake just below the top.

2 Roll out the white paste and use a palette knife to cut a large piece of paste with a wavy edge. Use the plunger cutter to cut two holes for eyes just below the centre point.

Cut two or three holes overlapping to create an oval mouth. Drape over the cupcake with the face over the black paste. Smooth and then lift the two pleats on either side upwards and outwards to create arms, adding a little sugar glue underneath to hold in place.

chain gang...
To make chains for your ghosts to clunk, roll little strips of grey paste and loop into circles, then paint with silver lustre dust mixed with clear alcohol.

Recipes cupcake • topping **Techniques** applying frostings • using sugarpaste

Difficulty rating:

Witches' hats

Add to the spell-binding scene with these bewitching cupcakes in the form of wonderfully wizened and wicked witches' hats.

you will need... makes 12

(12 cupcakes, flat frosted

(sugarpaste (rolled fondant) with CMC: 1kg (2lb 4oz) deep purple (M & B) and 200g (7oz) navy blue (RI) blended together, 30g (1oz) teddy bear brown

(gold lustre dust mixed with gin or vodka, or isopropyl alcohol

(sugar glue

(cutters: star plunger set (PME), 1.4cm (⅜in) circle

1 For the brims, roll out the blended purple and navy paste to 3mm (⅛in) thick using spacers. Use a circle cutter to cut 12 circles slightly larger than the cake cases to sit on top of them.

2 Roll a ball of the paste, then angle your hand down at the outer edge and roll to create a cone. Stand upright, smooth downwards and create a flat bottom with a sharp edge. Hold the cone over the brim to check that it's not too large in proportion. Attach with sugar glue. Use a palette knife to make a few cuts to 'distress' the hat and bend over the top.

3 Use the star cutters to cut out different-size brown paste stars, about 10 per cake. Use the circle cutter to cut three circles per cake, then cut again with the cutter into crescents. Attach to the hat randomly with sugar glue. Paint the shapes with the gold lustre dust solution.

black magic...
We love this fun purple hat, but you could make a more traditional black one and decorate with stars painted with silver lustre dust solution instead.

Recipes cupcake • topping **Techniques** applying frostings • using sugarpaste

Christmas

Each of these cupcake designs focuses on a classic festive motif but is executed in a new and fun way. Cone-shaped Christmas trees, the fluffy fur of Santa's hat and the handsome heads of his reindeer are all created with piping, while domes of chocolate frosting and cutters are used to make delightful plum puddings.

Design inspiration ideas

Once you're in the festive mood, there are lots more Christmassy cupcakes that you can enjoy creating. Take Rudolph's nose as inspiration, for instance, and roll paste into balls and then decorate with edible shimmering flakes or paint with lustre dusts to make some dazzling baubles. Or mould gift or cracker shapes from festive-coloured paste and decorate with strips of paste wound around a stick for curly ribbon trimmings.

Difficulty rating:

Oh Christmas tree

Set the festive party scene with these lovely little trees, decorated just like real Christmas trees with miniature candy canes, shiny baubles and a dazzling star on the top.

you will need... makes 12

- ☆ 12 cupcakes, flat frosted

- ☆ sugarpaste (rolled fondant) with CMC: 20g (¾oz) each yellow, red and white

- ☆ 600g (1lb 5oz) Christmas Green and Green Extra (SF)-coloured vanilla buttercream

- ☆ silver or multicoloured dragées (sugar balls)

- ☆ star plunger cutter set (PME)

- ☆ no. 1B drop (WIL) piping tube (tip)

1 Use the large star plunger cutter from the set to cut out 12 stars from the thinly rolled-out yellow paste. Set aside to firm.

2 For the candy canes, first roll a fine rope of both red and white paste. Lay them next to each other and, starting at one end, roll them forwards while sliding your hand forward and to the right so that they begin to twist together. Cut smaller sections and roll them so that the colours blend together, then cut a 2cm (¾in) length and bend one end into a curve.

3 For the tree, fill a large disposable plastic piping (pastry) bag fitted with the no. 1B drop tube with the deep green buttercream and pipe a small squirt of buttercream into the centre of each cake. Leaving a little of the cake showing around the edge, start piping from the outside, applying pressure, and work in a circular motion inwards and upwards to create a tall, tree-like swirl.

4 Add a yellow star to the top of each tree, three candy canes around the mid-section and then dot around several silver or multicoloured dragées – all the decorations will stick to the freshly piped buttercream.

cover up...
If you would rather not show the cake bases, cover your cakes with sugarpaste before you pipe on the trees.

Recipes cupcake • topping   Techniques applying frostings • using sugarpaste

Difficulty rating:

Rudolph and friends

A team of jolly festive reindeers are great for kids to create – to make it easy for them, use pretzels for antlers, a red sweet for Rudolph's nose and chocolate buttons for his buddies' noses.

you will need... makes 12

☆ 12 cupcakes, unfrosted

☆ 50g (1¾oz) Bulrush Brown (SK) flower (petal/gum) paste

☆ sugarpaste (rolled fondant) with CMC: 20g (¾oz) white, 20g (¾oz) blue, 10g (¼oz) black, 10g (¼oz) red, 110g (4oz) chocolate brown

☆ red edible shimmering flakes

☆ 600g (1lb 5oz) chocolate frosting

☆ sugar glue

☆ cutters: antler (C4F), oval set (C4F), 1.4cm (⅝in) circle

☆ no. 848 closed star piping tube (tip)

and for the plum puddings...

☆ 12 cupcakes with half-sphere dome of chocolate frosting

☆ sugarpaste (rolled fondant) with CMC: 100g (3½oz) white, 30g (1oz) green, 20g (¾oz) red

☆ sugar glue

☆ cutters: large 5-petal flower, small three-leaf holly plunger (PME)

1 Roll out the brown flower paste thinly and use the antler cutter to cut 12 antlers from each side of the cutter. Set aside to dry.

2 For the eyes, use the largest oval cutter to cut white paste ovals, then use the next size cutter to impress an oval inside each to create a line. Use the next size cutter to cut out blue paste ovals. Attach to the white ones near the base. For the pupils, use the next size cutter to cut out black paste ovals and attach as pupils. Use the smallest cutter to cut three white paste ovals and then cut them into thin triangular slithers. Use the tip of a slightly moist paintbrush to pick up the slivers and attach to the pupils to give the reindeers a glint in their eyes.

3 For Rudolph's nose, roll the red paste into a ball. Paint with sugar glue and dip into red shimmering flakes. Roll chocolate brown paste noses for the other reindeers.

think ahead...
Make the antlers a day or several days in advance to allow them to dry out and become as strong as possible.

4 For the reindeer head, fill a large disposable plastic piping (pastry) bag fitted with the no. 848 star piping tube with the chocolate frosting and pipe a small squirt of frosting into the centre of each cake. Then applying pressure, start piping from the outside and work in a circular motion inwards and upwards to create a high swirl.

5 Place a nose on each head and then the eyes. Position the antlers either side towards the top of the head – all the decorations will stick to the freshly piped buttercream.

for the plum pudding cakes

1 Use the 5-petal flower cutter to cut out 12 flower shapes from the thinly rolled-out white paste. Use a mini palette knife to lift and position a flower onto the top of each dome-frosted cake.

2 For the holly sprigs, use the holly plunger cutter to cut 12 sets of holly leaves from the thinly rolled-out green paste. Roll three tiny balls of red paste as berries for each set of leaves. Attach the leaves and berries to the centres of the white flowers with sugar glue.

Recipes cupcake • topping **Techniques** applying frostings • using sugarpaste

Festive favourites

Difficulty rating:

Complete your Christmas table with these cupcakes fashioned as that endearing festive accessory, Santa's fur-trimmed hat.

you will need... makes 12

- ☆ 12 cupcakes, unfrosted
- ☆ 600g (1lb 5oz) Red Extra (5F)-coloured vanilla buttercream
- ☆ 200g (7oz) white royal icing with ½ tsp (2.5ml) glycerine
- ☆ piping tubes (tips): no. 808 open round, no. 16 (Ateco)
- ☆ paper piping (pastry) bag

1 Fill a large disposable plastic piping (pastry) bag fitted with the no. 808 open round piping tube with the deep red buttercream and pipe a small squirt into the centre of each unfrosted cake. Then applying pressure, start piping from the outside and work in a circular motion inwards and upwards to create a cone.

2 For the pom-pom, fill the paper piping bag fitted with the no. 16 piping tube with the white royal icing and pipe a few practice elongated fluffy stars onto paper. When you are feeling confident, pipe one on the top of each hat cone. Then pipe a fluffy star trimming around the base of each cake.

festive sparkle...
As a finishing touch for the Santa's hats, sprinkle over some clear edible shimmering flakes to give them some festive sparkle.

Recipes cupcake • topping **Techniques** applying frostings • using sugarpaste

About the author

Carolyn has always loved having fun with cakes, hence her company name Cakes 4 Fun! Everything she looks at is stored away as 'that could make a great cake one day', and this is just how she sees everything, from a handbag to a greetings card.

She started her cake-making business at home following redundancy and quickly grew it through her passion for fun novelty cakes and her eye for detail. The business has grown gradually and she has always welcomed new people to join it, enjoying sharing her techniques with fellow team members and learning from their varied experiences to help her continually keep the company fresh and exciting. From her Putney-based shop and online store, her cake business now encompasses novelty cakes, wedding and corporate cakes, cake-decorating supplies and a thriving tutoring enterprise teaching cake enthusiasts every style of cake decorating from cupcakes to 3D designer handbags.

Carolyn has also written *Cupcake Fun* and *Cake Pops* in the *Bake Me I'm Yours…* series, so if you like this book, why not try your hand at creating some more cupcake designs or cake pops!

Acknowledgments

Many thanks to the whole David & Charles team for their amazing professional approach, enthusiasm and support throughout the whole process – special thanks to James, Grace, Jennifer and Jo, and I would also like to say a special thanks to members of the Cakes 4 Fun team: my fellow cupcake enthusiast Samantha Harrison who joined me in the fun side of designing and creating the great cupcake ideas in this book. Also thanks to Simone Clarke, my operations manager, and her fantastic cake team that whizzed up the many recipes, road-tested them and helped with producing brilliant cakes for the final shoot. Thanks also to Sam's sons who made a great cake-tasting panel – Stevie, Adam and Danny always gave their honest opinion and munched their way through many a cupcake in the course of this book!

I would also like to thank Graham, my husband, without whose inspiration, support and time spent distracting the kids while I was working to deadlines this book would never have existed.

Suppliers

UK

Cakes 4 Fun
100 Lower Richmond Road,
Putney, London SW15 1LN
Tel: 020 8785 9039
www.cakes4funshop.co.uk
Bespoke cake creations, sugarcraft shop and online
shop stocking all cake-making equipment used in
this book; sugarcraft school teaching all forms of
cake decoration.

RUCraft
www.rucraft.co.uk/thepinkwhisk
Tel: 0844 880 5852
All the cake-decorating and baking equipment to
get you started – and lots more besides!

Keylink Ltd
Green Lane, Ecclesfield,
Sheffield, S35 9WY
Tel: 01142 455400
www.keylink.org
Suppliers of Belgian Callebaut chocolate callets and
clear presentation boxes.

Knightsbridge PME Ltd
Unit 23, Riverwalk Road
(off Jeffreys Road),
Enfield EN3 7QN
Tel: 020 323 40049
www.cakedecoration.co.uk
Suppliers of plunger cutters, modelling tools and
cake stands, and UK distributor of Wilton Industries
products.

US

Global Sugar Art
625 Route 3, Unit 3,
Plattsburgh, NY 12901
Tel: + 1 518 561 3039
www.globalsugarart.com
Sugarcraft suppliers that also import many UK
products into the USA.

Kemper Enterprises Inc
13595 12th Street,
Chino, CA 91710
Tel: + 1 909 627 6191
www.kempertools.com
For mini plunger cutters and palette knives – also
available through all good cake-decorating stores.

Wilton Industries
2240 West 75th Street,
Woodridge, IL 60517
Tel: + 1 800 794 5866
www.wilton.com
For cupcake cases (liners) and cake stands.

Abbreviations used in this book

C4F – Cakes 4 Fun
PME – PME Sugarcraft
RI – Regalice
SF – Sugarflair
SK – Squires Kitchen
WIL – Wilton

NB All sugarpaste (rolled fondant)
colours used in the book are either
Regalice or M & B

I would like to dedicate this book to:
Jamie and Ella, who love cupcakes –
particularly the icing!

Index

A DAVID & CHARLES BOOK
© F&W Media International, Ltd 2012

David & Charles is an imprint of F&W Media International, Ltd
Brunel House, Forde Close, Newton Abbot, TQ12 4PU, UK

F&W Media International, Ltd is a subsidiary of F+W Media, Inc
10151 Carver Road, Suite #200, Blue Ash, OH 45242, USA

Text and Designs © Carolyn White 2012
Layout and Photography © F&W Media International, Ltd 2012

First published in the UK and USA in 2012

Carolyn White has asserted her right to be identified
as author of this work in accordance with the
Copyright, Designs and Patents Act, 1988.

Names of manufacturers and product ranges are
provided for the information of readers, with no
intention to infringe copyright or trademarks.

A catalogue record for this book is
available from the British Library.

ISBN-13: 978-1-4463-0301-6 paperback
ISBN-10: 1-4463-0301-2 paperback

Printed in China by RR Donnelley for:
F&W Media International, Ltd
Brunel House, Forde Close, Newton Abbot, TQ12 4PU, UK

10 9 8 7 6 5 4 3 2 1

Junior Acquisitions Editor: James Brooks
Assistant Editor: Grace Harvey
Project Editor: Jo Richardson
Junior Designer: Jennifer Stanley
Photographer: Sian Irvine
Senior Production Controller: Kelly Smith

F+W Media publishes high-quality books
on a wide range of subjects.
For more great book ideas visit: www.rucraft.co.uk